WELSH WORDS OF WISDOM

Inspirational proverbs from Wales

First impression: 2025

Cover, design & illustrations Tanwen Haf
Illustrations © Tanwen Haf
Text © Garmon Gruffudd

ISBN: 9781800997370

Published and printed in Wales
on paper from well-maintained forests by
Y Lolfa Cyf., Talybont, Ceredigion SY24 5HE
website www.ylolfa.com
e-mail ylolfa@ylolfa.com
tel 01970 832 304

WELSH WORDS OF WISDOM

Inspirational proverbs from Wales

y olfa

Foreword

Be it rugby, football, or politics, people often speak of a 'Welsh way' of doing things. In these pages, you'll find a collection of Welsh proverbs, quotes, and folk wisdom that offer guidance on how to live life the 'Welsh way'. Whether humorous, heartfelt, or sharply insightful, these expressions reveal enduring truths about life, love, work, and human nature. Some are uniquely Welsh, others more universal—but many have become deeply rooted in our language, culture and way of life.

Garmon Gruffudd

Note

Please note that the translations are not always literal: sometimes a roughly equivalent English proverb has been used. They are listed in alphabetical order for ease of reference.

Pronunciation

Every letter in Welsh is pronounced – there are no silent letters as in English. Most letters have only one basic sound, which makes pronunciation simple, but you will notice that all vowels can be long or short. The accent is usually on the last syllable but one. Here is the Welsh alphabet with equivalent English sounds:

A – as in h*a*rd or h*a*m
B – b
C – k
CH – as in Ba*ch*, the composer
D – d
DD – as in *th*em
E – as in s*a*ne or s*e*lf
F – v
FF – ff
G – as in *g*arden
NG – as in lo*ng*
H – as in *h*at
I – as in t*ea* or t*i*n
J – j
L – l
LL – as in *Ll*ane*ll*i. Place the tongue on the roof of the mouth as if to pronounce L, then blow voicelessly
M – m
N – n
O – as in *o*re
P – p
PH – ff
R – r
RH – rh
S – as in *s*ong, never as in a*s*
T – t
TH – as in clo*th*
U – roughly like Welsh i
W – as in b*oo*n or c*oo*k
Y – as in t*ea* or t*i*n or r*u*n

A deithio mewn cariad,
nid mwy mil milltir nag un.

For he who journeys for love,
a thousand miles is not more than one.

A ddarlleno, ystyried;
A ystyrio, cofied;
A gofio, gwnaed;
A wnêl, parhaed.

He who reads, consider;
He who considers, remember;
He who remembers, act;
He who acts, persevere.

– Ellis Wynne

A ddwg wy a ddwg fwy.

He who steals one egg will steal more.

A ddywed y peth a fynno,
a glyw y peth nis mynno.

He who says what he likes
will hear what he doesn't like.

A fo ben bid bont.

He who leads must be a bridge.

– Y Mabinogion

A fo fwyaf ei awydd,
mwyaf oll ei siom a fydd.

The more his eagerness,
the greater his sorrow will be.

– Dic Jones

A fynno ddrwg i'w gymydog,
iddo'i hun y daw.

He who wishes ill on his neighbour,
ill will come to him.

A fynno glod, bid farw.

He who seeks glory must die first.

A fynno iechyd, bid lawen.

He who wants health, let him be happy.

A ŵyr leiaf a ddywed fwyaf.

Empty vessels make the most sound.

Lit.: He who knows least will speak most.

Adar o'r unlliw ehedant i'r unlle.

Birds of a feather flock together.

Adfyd a ddwg wybodaeth,
a gwybodaeth ddoethineb.

*Adversity brings knowledge,
and knowledge wisdom.*

Angau'r euog ydyw'r gwir.

Truth is the death of the guilty.

Angel pen ffordd, diawl pen pentan.

An angel in public, a devil at home.

Angen yw mam pob celfyddyd.

Necessity is the mother of invention.

Allan o'r golwg, allan o'r meddwl.

Out of sight, out of mind.

Anodd tynnu cast o hen geffyl.

It is difficult to cure an old horse of a bad habit.

Aros mae'r mynyddau mawr,
Rhuo drostynt mae y gwynt.

Still do the great mountains stay,
And the winds above them roar.

– Ceiriog (trans. Tony Conran)

Benthyg dros amser byr
yw popeth a geir yn y byd hwn.

All wordly possessions are on a short term loan.

Boddi a wna'r dyn na nofia
yn erbyn llif y wlad.

He will drown, who does not swim
against the country's tide.

– Morgan Llwyd

Brodyr pob cerddorion.

All musicians are brothers.

Buan i'r wledd, buan i'r bedd.

Early to the feast, early to the grave.

Bûm gall unwaith –
hynny oedd llefain pan y'm ganed.
I was wise once – that I cried when I was born.

Byddwch lawen, cadwch y ffydd,
a gwnewch y pethau bychain
a welsoch ac a glywsoch gennyf i.
Be joyful, keep the faith,
and do the little things
you saw and heard from me.
– Dewi Sant, patron saint of Wales

Cais y doeth ragori arno'i hun;
cais yr annoeth ragori ar eraill.
The wise man seeks to surpass himself;
the foolish man to surpass others.

Cân di bennill mwyn i'th nain,
fe gân dy nain i tithau.

Praise me, praise thee.

*Lit.: Sing your grandma a sweet song
and your gran shall sing for you.*

Câr dy gymydog ond cadw dy glawdd.

Love your neighbour but don't pull down your hedge.

Caredigrwydd gŵr mawr a lleuad lawn,
nid ydynt ond daioni diwrnod.

*A great man's generosity and a full moon
are good for one day only.*

Cariad a heddwch, brodyr ydynt.

Love and peace are brothers.

Cartref yw cartref, er tloted y bo.

Home is where the heart is.

Lit.: Home is home, no matter how poor it is.

Cas gŵr na charo'r wlad a'i maco.

Hateful the man who does not love the country that nurtured him.

Cenedl heb iaith, cenedl heb galon.

A nation without a language is a nation without a heart.

Cwrw da yw allwedd calon.

Good beer is the key to the heart.

Cwsg galar ond ni chwsg gofid.

Mourning sleeps but anxiety does not.

Cwsg yw bywyd heb lyfrau.

A life without books is a dormant life.

Cyfaill blaidd, bugail diog.

A wolf's best friend is a lazy shepherd.

Cyfrinach llwyddiant yw diwydrwydd.

Diligence is the key to success.

Cyngor doeth,
gwell nag aur coeth.

Wise advice is worth
more than pure gold.

Cynt y cwrdd dau ddyn
na dau fynydd.

Sooner will two men meet
than two mountains.

Chwerthin yw moddion
afiechydon fil.

Laughter is the best medicine
for a thousand illnesses.

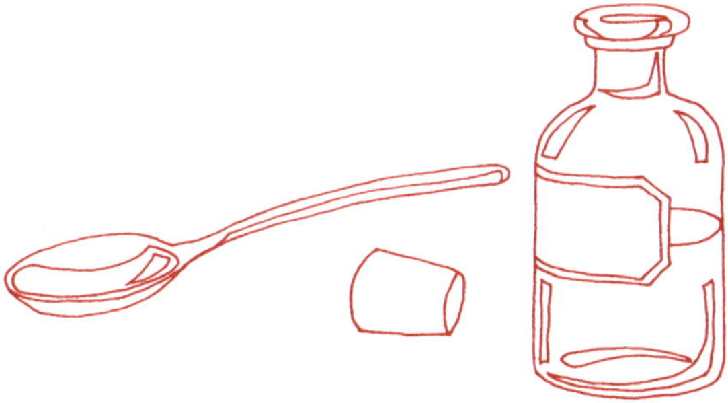

Chwilia rhai am hapusrwydd uwch na dyn,
eraill am hapusrwydd is na dyn –
ond mae hapusrwydd yr un faint â dyn.

Some seek happiness greater than man,
others happiness lower than man –
but happiness is the same size as man.

Chwynnwch eich gardd
eich hun yn gyntaf.

Weed your own garden first.

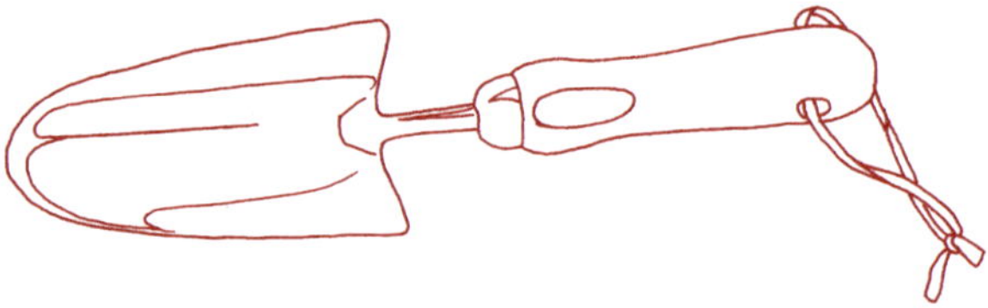

Da am dda sy dra rhesymol,
Drwg am ddrwg sydd anghristnogol,
Drwg am dda sydd yn gythreulig,
Da am ddrwg sy fendigedig.

Good for good is very reasonable,
Bad for bad is not commendable,
Bad for good is unforgivable,
Good for bad is quite adorable.

Da yw dweud ond gwell yw gwneud.

Actions speak louder than words.

Daw dydd y bydd mawr y rhai bychain,
daw dydd ni bydd mwy y rhai mawr.

The day will come when the small shall be great,
the day will come when the great shall be no more.

– Waldo Williams

Deuparth gwaith ei ddechrau.

Work begun is half done.

Lit.: Starting is two-thirds of the work.

Digon i'r diwrnod ei ddrwg ei hun.

Sufficient to the day its own misfortune.

Digon yw ychydig yn
rhagor nag sydd gennyt.

Enough is a little more
than you already have.

Digrif gan bob aderyn ei lais ei hun.

Every bird fancies its own voice.

Diwedd pob trais, tristwch.

Violence always ends in sorrow.

Diwedd y gân yw'r geiniog.

It all comes down to money.
Lit.: The end of the song is the penny.

Doeth a newid ei farn,
ffôl a'i ceidw'n gadarn.

*Wise men change their minds,
fools never do.*

Duw a'm gwaredo,
ni allaf ddianc rhag hon.

*God help me,
I cannot escape from her (Wales).*

– T. H. Parry-Williams

Dyfal donc a dyr y garreg.

Practice makes perfect.

Lit.: Persistence will break the stone.

Dywed yn dda am dy gyfaill;
am dy elyn dywed ddim.

Speak well of your friend;
of your enemy say nothing.

Enfys y bore,
Aml gawode;
Enfys y pnawn,
Tegwch a gawn.

A rainbow in the morning,
Showers to come;
A rainbow in the afternoon,
Fair weather and sun.

Gair i ddoeth, cant i annoeth.

A word for the wise, a hundred for the unwise.

Gall pechod mawr ddyfod trwy ddrws bychan.

A great sin can enter through a small door.

Gan y gwirion y ceir y gwir.

From a fool you'll get the truth.

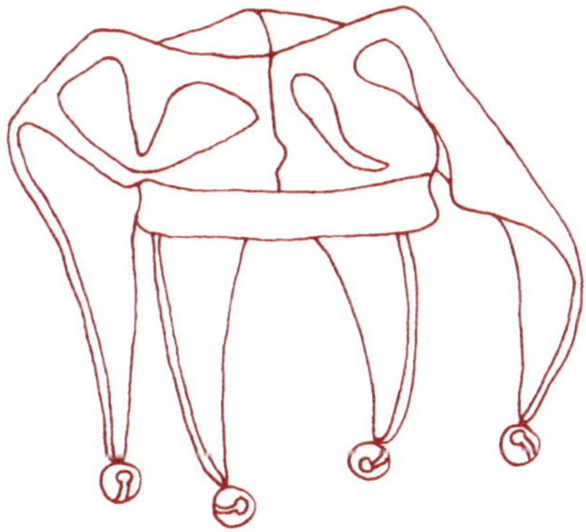

Gellir adnabod dyn wrth ei gyfeillion.

You can tell a man by his friends.

Gorau arf, arf dysg.

Learning is the best weapon.

Gorau cannwyll, pwyll i ddyn.

The best candle for a man is a cool head.

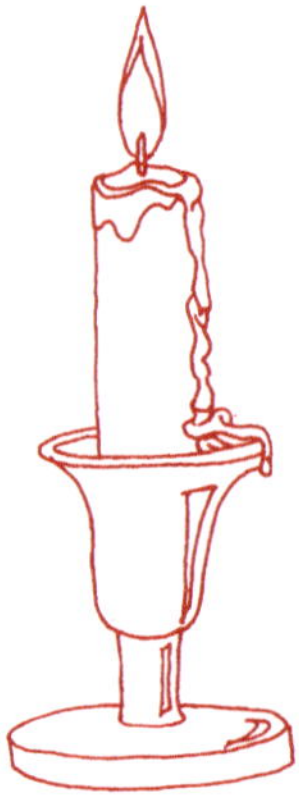

Gorau cyfoeth yw iechyd.

Health is the greatest treasure.

Gorau Cymro, Cymro oddi cartref.

The best Welshman is a Welshman abroad.

Gorau chwarae cydchwarae.

Together stronger.

– motto of the Welsh national football team

Gorau meddyg, amser.

Time is the best healer.

Gorau prinder, prinder geiriau.

The best shortage is a shortage of words.

Gormod o ddim nid yw dda.

Too much of anything is good for nothing.

Gormod o ryddid a dry'n gaethiwed.

Too much freedom leads to servitude.

Gwae chwi pan ddywedo
pob dyn yn dda amdanoch.

Woe betide the man of whom all say only good.

Gwasanaeth Duw yw gwneuthur iawn –
Nid gweddïo bore a nawn.

God is served by doing right –
Not by praying day and night.

Gwell aderyn mewn llaw
na dau mewn llwyn.

A bird in the hand is worth two in the bush.

Gwell dysg na golud.

Learning is better than wealth.

Gwell fy mwthyn fy hun na phlas arall.

Better my own cottage than another's mansion.

Gwell hwyr na hwyrach.

Better late than never.

Gwell llaeth Cymru na chwrw Lloegr.

Better Welsh milk than English beer.

– Eirwyn Pontshân

Gwell moes na bonedd.

High morals are better than a high lineage.

Gwell nag athro yw arfer.

Practice is the best teacher.

Gwell yr heddwch gwaethaf na'r rhyfel gorau.

Better the worst peace than the best war.

Gwell yw anelu at rywbeth a'i fethu nag anelu at ddim a'i daro.

It's better to aim at something and fail than to aim at nothing and succeed.

Gwell yw cymydog yn agos na brawd ymhell.

Better a nearby neighbour than a brother afar.

Gŵr heb bwyll, llong heb angor.

A rash man is like an anchorless ship.

Gwyn eu byd yr adar gwylltion,
Hwy gânt fynd i'r fan a fynnon',
Weithie i'r môr ac weithie i'r mynydd,
A dŵad gartref yn ddigerydd.

Blessed are the wild birds
Who fly where they wish,
Sometimes to the sea
and sometimes to the mountains,
And return home without rebuke.

Gwyn y gwêl y frân ei chyw.

The raven sees its chick as white.

Hawdd clwyfo claf.

It's easy to wound an ill person.

Hawdd cynnau tân ar hen aelwyd.

It's easy to rekindle an old flame.

Hawdd yw dwedyd 'Dacw'r Wyddfa!'
Nid eir trosti ond yn ara'.

It's easy to say, 'There's Snowdon!'
But slow the climb to its peak.

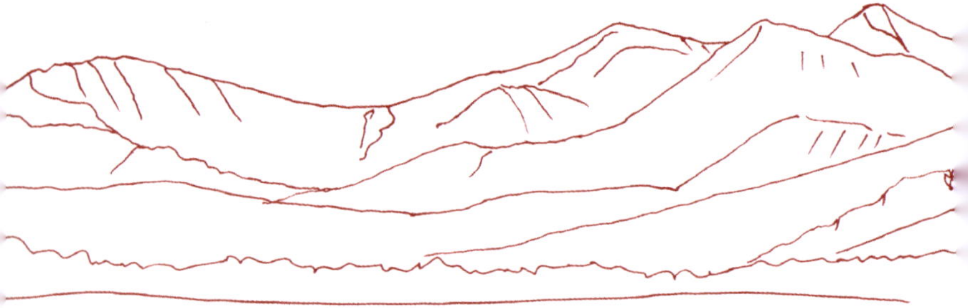

Haws cau llygad na chau ceg.

It's easier to see nothing than to say nothing.

Heb ddysg, heb ddawn,
Heb ddawn, heb ddoethineb,
Heb ddoethineb, heb Dduw,
Heb Dduw, heb ddim; Duw a digon.

Without learning, without talent,
Without talent, without wisdom,
Without wisdom, without God,
Without God, nothing; with God, plenty.

Heb ei fai, heb ei eni.

Nobody's perfect.

Lit.: He who has no faults is not yet born.

"Hed amser," meddi.

Na, erys amser, dyn a â.

"Time flies," you say.

No, time remains, it's man that goes.

Hedyn pob drwg yw diogi.

Laziness is the seed of all evil.

Henaint ni ddaw ei hunan.

Old age does not come alone.

Hir ei dafod, byr ei wybod.

Long of tongue, short on knowledge.

Hir pob aros.

The watched kettle never boils.

Lit.: All waiting is long.

Hoff pob gwaharddedig.

Everything forbidden is craved.

Hysbys y dengys y dyn
O ba radd y bo'i wreiddyn.

A man soon reveals
The grade of his roots.

– Tudur Aled

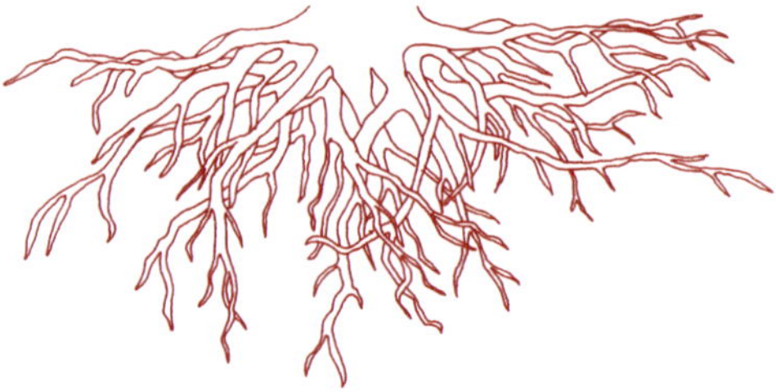

I'r pant y rhed y dŵr.

Money goes where money is.
Lit.: The water runs into the hollow.

Iachaf croen, croen cachgi.

The healthiest skin is that of a coward.

Llais deilen yn y gwynt
a darf gydwybod euog.

*The rustle of a leaf in the wind will
disturb a guilty conscience.*

Lle bo camp bydd rhemp.

Where there is excellence, there is depravity.

Mae arian yn was da ond yn feistr drwg.

Money is a good servant but a poor master.

Mae cybydd bob amser mewn angen.

A miser is always in need.

Mae chwarae'n troi'n chwerw
wrth chwarae â thân.

Playing with fire will end in tears.
Lit.: Play turns bitter when you play with fire.

Mae llathed o gownter
yn well na chan cyfer o dir.

A yard of counter
is better than a hundred acres of land.

Mae methiant yn well athro na llwyddiant.

Failure is a better teacher than success.

Mae mistar ar Fistar Mostyn.

There's a boss for every boss.
Lit.: Even Mr Mostyn has a master.

Man gwyn man draw.

The grass is always greener on the other side.

Melys moes mwy.

Sweetness craves more.

Melysaf y cân eos,
ond nid erchis Duw i'r frân dewi.

The nightingale sings sweetest,
but God did not order the crow to stop cawing.

Mewn undeb mae nerth.

Strength lies in unity.

Mwya'r brys, mwya'r rhwystr.

More haste, less speed.

Mynych fenter, aml golled.

Many ventures, frequent losses.

Na ddeffro'r ci sy'n cysgu.

Let sleeping dogs lie.

Na farnwch fel na'ch bernir.

Do not judge or you'll be judged yourself.

Nac ofnwch farwolaeth y corff,
eithr marwolaeth yr ysbryd.

Do not fear the death of the body,
but the death of the spirit.

Nesaf i'r eglwys, pellaf o baradwys.

The nearer to the church, the further from paradise.

Ni feddwl, ni ailfeddwl.

He who does not think does not rethink.

Ni fu colled i neb na fu'n ennill i rywun.

There was never a loss that wasn't someone's gain.

Nid ar redeg mae aredig.

Slow and steady wins the race.

Lit.: Ploughing cannot be done on the run.

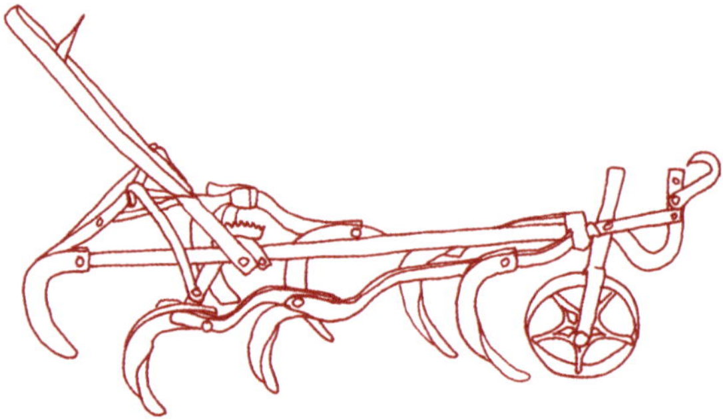

Nid aur yw popeth melyn.

All that glitters is not gold.

Nid colled colli yr hyn ni chawd.

It's no loss to lose what you never had.

Nid da lle gellir gwell.

There's always room for improvement.

Lit.: It's not good if it can be done better.

Nid da rhy o ddim.

Too much of anything is not good.

Nid oes ar uffern ond angen ei threfnu.

Hell only needs to be organized.

Nid oes neb mor ddall
â'r neb ni fynno weled.

There is none so blind
as he who will not see.

Nid twyll twyllo twyllwr.

It's not deceitful to deceive a deceiver.

Nid ydyw Duw mor greulon
Ag y dywaid hen ddynion.

God isn't as cruel
As old men tell.

– Dafydd ap Gwilym

Nid yn y bore mae canmol diwrnod teg.

The morning isn't the time to praise a fine day.

Nid yw geiriau gwir yn brydferth,
nid yw geiriau prydferth yn wir.

True words are not beautiful,
beautiful words are not true.

O flewyn i flewyn
yr â'r pen yn foel.

Hair by hair
does the head grow bare.

O gyfoeth y daw gofid.

From wealth comes sorrow.

Oferedd yw printio llawer o lyfrau; blinder yw cynnwys llawer o feddyliau; peryglus yw dywedyd llawer o eiriau; anghysurus yw croesawu llawer o ysbrydoedd, a ffolineb yw ceisio ateb holl resymau dynion: ond, O ddyn, cais di adnabod dy galon dy hun, a mynd i mewn i'r porth cyfyng.

It is vain to print many books; it is tiresome to contain many thoughts; it is perilous to speak many words; it is discomforting to welcome many spirits, and foolish to try and answer all of men's reasons: but, Oh man, seek to know your own heart, and enter through the narrow gate.

– Morgan Llwyd

Os nad wyt gryf, bydd gyfrwys.

If you're not strong, be smart.

Pa lesâd i ddyn os cyll efe yr holl fyd,
ac ennill ei enaid ei hun?

*What will it profit a man if he loses the whole world,
and gains his own soul?*

– Welsh playwright, W.S. Jones

Pa werth na thry yn wawd
pan laddo dyn ei frawd?

*What values do not turn to dust (lit. mockery)
when a man kills his brother?*

– Waldo Williams

Pan gaiff dyn ei fesur,
gofynnir gan Dduw
Nid sut y gwnaeth farw,
ond sut y gwnaeth fyw.

When man will be measured,
God will enquire
Not how did he die,
but how did he live.

– John Gwilym Jones

Pan gyll y call, fe gyll ymhell.

When a wise man goes astray, he strays far.

Pawb â'i fys lle bo'i ddolur.

Each has a finger on his own bruise.

Pawb drosto ei hun, a Duw dros bawb.

Each man for himself, and God for all.

Po ddyfnaf yr afon, lleiaf oll ei thrwst.

The deeper the river, the quieter its roar.

Po fwyaf y cwsg, hwyaf yr einioes.

The more you sleep, the longer you live.

Pob ffôl a wna offeiriad.

Any fool can become a priest.

Rhaid cropian cyn cerdded.

You must walk before you run.

Lit.: You must crawl before you walk.

Rhwydd ei gael, rhwydd ei golli.

Easy come, easy go.

Rhy hwyr codi pais ar ôl piso.

It's too late to lift your petticoat after you've peed.

Rhydd i bawb ei farn,
ac i bob barn ei llafar.

All have a right to their opinion,
and all opinions their voice.

Segurdod yw clod y cledd,
A rhwd yw ei anrhydedd.

Idleness is the glory of the sword,
And rust its nobility.

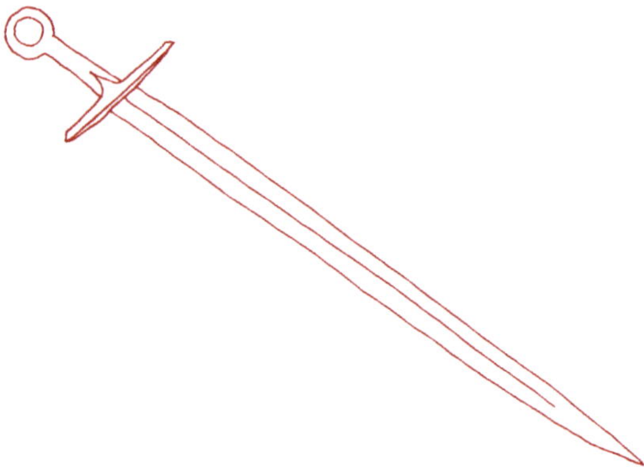

Trech gwlad nag arglwydd.

The people are mightier than the lord.

Trechaf treisied, gwannaf gwaedded.

The strong will crush and the weak will squeal.

Tri chynnig i Gymro.

Three tries for a Welshman.

Tri pheth a newidiant yn fynych:
y lleuad, y gwynt, a meddwl gwraig.

Three things that often change:
the moon, the wind, and a woman's mind.

Un wennol ni wna wanwyn.

One swallow does not a summer (lit. spring) make.

Unwaith yn ddyn, dwywaith yn blentyn.

Once a man, twice a child.

Wrth gicio a brathu mae cariad yn magu.

While kicking and biting, love develops.

Y cyntaf i'r felin gaiff falu.

The early bird catches the worm.

Lit.: The first to the mill may grind.

Y cyw a fegir yn uffern,
yn uffern y myn fod.

A chick reared in hell
will want to stay in hell.

Y gwir yn erbyn y byd.

The truth against the world.

Y neb a bwyso ar hawddfyd
am ddedwyddwch sydd
yn gorwedd ar ddrain.

He who depends on easy times
for happiness lies on thorns.

– Llew Tegid

Y neb a orchfyga'i nwyd
a wiredda ei freuddwyd.

He who conquers his desires
will realise his dream.

– Dic Jones

Ym mhob braint y mae dyletswydd.

Every privilege carries an obligation.

Yn sydyn daw dydd Sadwrn.

Saturday comes round suddenly.

Yr euog a ffy heb ei erlid.

The guilty will flee without being chased.

Yr hen a ŵyr, yr ifanc a dybia.

The old know, the young presume.

Yr hyn a fu a fydd,
a'r hyn a wnaed a wneir:
nid oes dim newydd dan yr haul.

What has been will be again,
what has been done will be done again;
there is nothing new under the sun.

– Llyfr y Pregethwr /

The Book of the Preacher